ONE MORE TIME

written by Ben Farrell illustrated by Susan Keeter

HARCOURT BRACE & COMPANY

Orlando Atlanta Austin Boston San Francisco Chicago Dallas New York
Toronto London

"This big ride is the one for me," said Ben.

"This ride here is the one for me," said Trina.

"This little ride is the one for me," said Todd.

"You all can ride this one,"

said Mother.

"One more time!"